AgendasRX

Organized + Saving Lives

WEEKLY PLANNER

DATES/WEEK OF:

AgendasRX
Organized ~ Saving Lives

○ MONDAY

PRIORITIES

_____

_____

○ TUESDAY

_____

_____

_____

○ WEDNESDAY

TO DO

_____

_____

○ THURSDAY

_____

_____

_____

○ FRIDAY

_____

_____

_____

○ SATURDAY / SUNDAY

_____

_____

_____

DATES/WEEK OF:

AgendasRX
Organized - Saving Lives

_____

○ MONDAY

PRIORITIES

_____
_____
○ TUESDAY   _____
_____
_____
_____
_____
○ WEDNESDAY

TO DO

_____
_____
_____
○ THURSDAY   _____
_____
_____
_____
_____
○ FRIDAY   _____
_____
_____
_____
_____
○ SATURDAY / SUNDAY   _____
_____
_____
_____

DATES/WEEK OF:

AgendasRX

Organized — Saving Lives

_____

O MONDAY

PRIORITIES
_____
_____

O TUESDAY
_____
_____
_____

O WEDNESDAY

TO DO
_____

O THURSDAY
_____
_____
_____

O FRIDAY
_____
_____
_____

O SATURDAY / SUNDAY
_____
_____

DATES/WEEK OF:

AgendasRX
Organized – Saving Lives

_____

○ MONDAY

PRIORITIES
_____
_____

○ TUESDAY
_____
_____
_____

○ WEDNESDAY

TO DO
_____

○ THURSDAY
_____
_____
_____

○ FRIDAY
_____
_____
_____

○ SATURDAY / SUNDAY
_____
_____
_____

DATES/WEEK OF:

AgendasRX

Organized – Saving Lives

○ MONDAY

PRIORITIES

○ TUESDAY

○ WEDNESDAY

TO DO

○ THURSDAY

○ FRIDAY

○ SATURDAY / SUNDAY

DATES/WEEK OF:

AgendasRX
Organized – Saving Lives

_____

○ MONDAY

PRIORITIES
_____
_____
○ TUESDAY   _____
_____
_____

○ WEDNESDAY

TO DO
_____
_____
○ THURSDAY   _____
_____
_____

○ FRIDAY   _____
_____
_____

○ SATURDAY / SUNDAY   _____
_____
_____

DATES/WEEK OF:

AgendasRX
Organized ~ Saving Lives

○ MONDAY

PRIORITIES

_____
_____

○ TUESDAY
_____
_____
_____

○ WEDNESDAY

TO DO

_____
_____

○ THURSDAY
_____
_____
_____
_____

○ FRIDAY
_____
_____
_____

○ SATURDAY / SUNDAY
_____
_____

DATES/WEEK OF:

AgendasRX
Organized - Saving Lives

_____

○ MONDAY

PRIORITIES

_____
_____
○ TUESDAY
_____
_____
_____
_____

○ WEDNESDAY

TO DO

_____
_____
_____
○ THURSDAY
_____
_____
_____
_____
○ FRIDAY
_____
_____
_____
○ SATURDAY / SUNDAY
_____
_____
_____

DATES/WEEK OF:

AgendasRX
Organized – Saving Lives

O MONDAY

PRIORITIES

O TUESDAY

O WEDNESDAY

TO DO

O THURSDAY

O FRIDAY

O SATURDAY / SUNDAY

DATES/WEEK OF:

AgendasRX
Organized – Saving Lives

_____

○ MONDAY

_____

PRIORITIES
_____
_____

○ TUESDAY
_____
_____

_____

○ WEDNESDAY

TO DO
_____

_____
_____

○ THURSDAY
_____
_____

_____
_____

○ FRIDAY
_____
_____

_____
_____

○ SATURDAY / SUNDAY
_____
_____

_____
_____

DATES/WEEK OF:

AgendasRX
Organized – Saving Lives

○ MONDAY

PRIORITIES
_____
_____
○ TUESDAY _____
_____
_____

○ WEDNESDAY

TO DO
_____
_____
○ THURSDAY _____
_____
_____
_____

○ FRIDAY _____
_____
_____

○ SATURDAY / SUNDAY _____
_____
_____

DATES/WEEK OF:

AgendasRX
Organized – Saving Lives

_____

○ MONDAY

PRIORITIES

_____
_____

○ TUESDAY

_____
_____
_____

○ WEDNESDAY

TO DO

_____

○ THURSDAY

_____
_____
_____
_____

○ FRIDAY

_____
_____
_____

○ SATURDAY / SUNDAY

_____
_____
_____

DATES/WEEK OF:

AgendasRX
Organized - Saving Lives

O MONDAY

PRIORITIES

_____
_____
_____
_____

O TUESDAY

_____
_____
_____

O WEDNESDAY

TO DO

_____
_____

O THURSDAY

_____
_____
_____
_____

O FRIDAY

_____
_____
_____
_____

O SATURDAY / SUNDAY

_____
_____
_____

DATES/WEEK OF:

AgendasRX
Organized - Saving Lives

_____

○ MONDAY

PRIORITIES
_____
_____
○ TUESDAY
_____
_____
_____

○ WEDNESDAY

TO DO
_____
_____
○ THURSDAY
_____
_____
_____
_____

○ FRIDAY
_____
_____
_____
_____
○ SATURDAY / SUNDAY
_____
_____
_____

DATES/WEEK OF:

AgendasRX
Organized - Saving Lives

○ MONDAY

PRIORITIES

_____

_____

○ TUESDAY

_____

_____

_____

○ WEDNESDAY

TO DO

_____

_____

○ THURSDAY

_____

_____

_____

○ FRIDAY

_____

_____

_____

_____

○ SATURDAY / SUNDAY

_____

_____

_____

DATES/WEEK OF:

AgendasRX
Organized - Saving Lives

_____

○ MONDAY

PRIORITIES

_____

_____

○ TUESDAY

_____

_____

_____

○ WEDNESDAY

TO DO

_____

○ THURSDAY

_____

_____

_____

○ FRIDAY

_____

_____

_____

○ SATURDAY / SUNDAY

_____

_____

_____

DATES/WEEK OF:

AgendasRX

Organized – Saving Lives

⭕ MONDAY

PRIORITIES

_____

⭕ TUESDAY

_____

_____

_____

_____

⭕ WEDNESDAY

TO DO

_____

_____

⭕ THURSDAY

_____

_____

_____

⭕ FRIDAY

_____

_____

_____

⭕ SATURDAY / SUNDAY

_____

_____

DATES/WEEK OF:

AgendasRX
Organized – Saving Lives

○ MONDAY

_____

PRIORITIES
_____
_____

○ TUESDAY
_____
_____
_____

_____

○ WEDNESDAY

TO DO
_____
_____

○ THURSDAY
_____
_____
_____

_____

○ FRIDAY
_____
_____
_____

_____

○ SATURDAY / SUNDAY
_____
_____
_____

_____

DATES/WEEK OF:

AgendasRX
Organized — Saving Lives

○ MONDAY

_____

PRIORITIES

○ TUESDAY

_____

○ WEDNESDAY

TO DO

○ THURSDAY

○ FRIDAY

○ SATURDAY / SUNDAY

DATES/WEEK OF:

AgendasRX
Organized - Saving Lives

○ MONDAY

PRIORITIES

_____

_____

○ TUESDAY

_____

_____

_____

○ WEDNESDAY

TO DO

_____

○ THURSDAY

_____

_____

_____

_____

○ FRIDAY

_____

_____

_____

_____

○ SATURDAY / SUNDAY

_____

_____

_____

_____

DATES/WEEK OF:

AgendasRX
Organized - Saving Lives

○ MONDAY

PRIORITIES

_____

_____

○ TUESDAY

_____

_____

_____

○ WEDNESDAY

TO DO

_____

_____

○ THURSDAY

_____

_____

_____

_____

○ FRIDAY

_____

_____

_____

○ SATURDAY / SUNDAY

_____

_____

_____

DATES/WEEK OF:

AgendasRX
Organized – Saving Lives

_____

○ MONDAY

PRIORITIES
_____
_____

○ TUESDAY
_____
_____
_____

○ WEDNESDAY

TO DO
_____

○ THURSDAY
_____
_____
_____

○ FRIDAY
_____
_____
_____

○ SATURDAY / SUNDAY
_____
_____
_____

DATES/WEEK OF:

AgendasRX
Organized – Saving Lives

○ MONDAY

PRIORITIES

_____

_____

○ TUESDAY

_____

_____

_____

○ WEDNESDAY

TO DO

_____

_____

○ THURSDAY

_____

_____

_____

○ FRIDAY

_____

_____

_____

○ SATURDAY / SUNDAY

_____

_____

_____

DATES/WEEK OF:

AgendasRX
Organized – Saving Lives

○ MONDAY

PRIORITIES

○ TUESDAY

○ WEDNESDAY

TO DO

○ THURSDAY

○ FRIDAY

○ SATURDAY / SUNDAY

DATES/WEEK OF:

AgendasRX
Organized - Saving Lives

O MONDAY

PRIORITIES

O TUESDAY

O WEDNESDAY

TO DO

O THURSDAY

O FRIDAY

O SATURDAY / SUNDAY

DATES/WEEK OF:

AgendasRX

Organized ~ Saving Lives

○ MONDAY

○ TUESDAY

PRIORITIES

_____

_____

_____

_____

_____

○ WEDNESDAY

TO DO

_____

_____

○ THURSDAY

_____

_____

_____

_____

○ FRIDAY

_____

_____

_____

_____

○ SATURDAY / SUNDAY

_____

_____

_____

_____

DATES/WEEK OF:

AgendasRX
Organized – Saving Lives

○ MONDAY

PRIORITIES

_____

○ TUESDAY

_____

_____

_____

_____

○ WEDNESDAY

TO DO

_____

○ THURSDAY

_____

_____

_____

○ FRIDAY

_____

_____

_____

○ SATURDAY / SUNDAY

_____

_____

_____

DATES/WEEK OF:

AgendasRX
Organized – Saving Lives

O MONDAY

PRIORITIES

O TUESDAY

O WEDNESDAY

TO DO

O THURSDAY

O FRIDAY

O SATURDAY / SUNDAY

DATES/WEEK OF:

AgendasRX
Organized - Saving Lives

○ MONDAY

PRIORITIES

_____

_____

○ TUESDAY

_____

_____

_____

○ WEDNESDAY

TO DO

_____

_____

○ THURSDAY

_____

_____

_____

○ FRIDAY

_____

_____

_____

○ SATURDAY / SUNDAY

_____

_____

DATES/WEEK OF:

AgendasRX
Organized - Saving Lives

○ MONDAY

PRIORITIES

_____

_____

○ TUESDAY

_____

_____

_____

○ WEDNESDAY

TO DO

_____

○ THURSDAY

_____

_____

_____

_____

○ FRIDAY

_____

_____

_____

○ SATURDAY / SUNDAY

_____

_____

DATES/WEEK OF:

AgendasRX
Organized ~ Saving Lives

○ MONDAY

PRIORITIES

_____

_____

○ TUESDAY

_____

_____

_____

○ WEDNESDAY

TO DO

_____

_____

○ THURSDAY

_____

_____

_____

○ FRIDAY

_____

_____

_____

○ SATURDAY / SUNDAY

_____

_____

DATES/WEEK OF:

AgendasRX
Organized - Saving Lives

_____

○ MONDAY

                                    PRIORITIES
                                    _____
_____   _____
                                    _____
○ TUESDAY   _____
                                    _____
                                    _____
_____   _____

○ WEDNESDAY

                                    TO DO
                                    _____
_____   _____
                                    _____
○ THURSDAY   _____
                                    _____
                                    _____
_____   _____
                                    _____
○ FRIDAY   _____
                                    _____
                                    _____
                                    _____
_____   _____
                                    _____
○ SATURDAY / SUNDAY   _____
                                    _____
                                    _____
_____   _____

DATES/WEEK OF:

AgendasRX
Organized − Saving Lives

○ MONDAY

PRIORITIES

○ TUESDAY

○ WEDNESDAY

TO DO

○ THURSDAY

○ FRIDAY

○ SATURDAY / SUNDAY

DATES/WEEK OF:

AgendasRX
Organized – Saving Lives

_____

O MONDAY

                                    PRIORITIES
                                    _____
_____   _____
                                    _____
O TUESDAY   _____
                                    _____
                                    _____

_____

O WEDNESDAY

                                    TO DO
                                    _____
_____   _____
                                    _____
O THURSDAY   _____
                                    _____
                                    _____

_____   _____

O FRIDAY   _____
                                    _____
                                    _____
                                    _____
_____   _____

O SATURDAY / SUNDAY   _____
                                    _____
                                    _____
_____   _____

DATES/WEEK OF:

AgendasRX
Organized — Saving Lives

⊙ MONDAY

PRIORITIES

_____

_____

⊙ TUESDAY

_____

_____

_____

⊙ WEDNESDAY

TO DO

_____

_____

⊙ THURSDAY

_____

_____

_____

_____

⊙ FRIDAY

_____

_____

_____

⊙ SATURDAY / SUNDAY

_____

_____

DATES/WEEK OF:

AgendasRX
Organized – Saving Lives

_____

○ MONDAY

PRIORITIES

_____

_____

○ TUESDAY

_____

_____

_____

○ WEDNESDAY

TO DO

_____

○ THURSDAY

_____

_____

_____

○ FRIDAY

_____

_____

_____

○ SATURDAY / SUNDAY

_____

_____

_____

DATES/WEEK OF:

AgendasRX

Organized – Saving Lives

_____

○ MONDAY

PRIORITIES

_____

_____

_____

_____

○ TUESDAY

_____

_____

_____

_____

○ WEDNESDAY

TO DO

_____

_____

_____

_____

○ THURSDAY

_____

_____

_____

_____

○ FRIDAY

_____

_____

_____

_____

○ SATURDAY / SUNDAY

_____

_____

_____

_____

DATES/WEEK OF:

AgendasRX

Organized ~ Saving Lives

○ MONDAY

PRIORITIES

_____

_____

○ TUESDAY

_____

_____

_____

_____

○ WEDNESDAY

TO DO

_____

_____

○ THURSDAY

_____

_____

_____

_____

○ FRIDAY

_____

_____

_____

_____

○ SATURDAY / SUNDAY

_____

_____

_____

DATES/WEEK OF:

AgendasRX

Organized - Saving Lives

_____

○ MONDAY

PRIORITIES
_____
_____
○ TUESDAY
_____
_____
_____

○ WEDNESDAY

TO DO
_____
_____
○ THURSDAY
_____
_____
_____

○ FRIDAY
_____
_____
_____

○ SATURDAY / SUNDAY
_____
_____
_____

DATES/WEEK OF:

AgendasRX

Organized ~ Saving Lives

⊙ MONDAY

_____

PRIORITIES

_____
_____

⊙ TUESDAY

_____
_____
_____

_____

⊙ WEDNESDAY

_____

TO DO

_____
_____

⊙ THURSDAY

_____
_____
_____

_____
_____

⊙ FRIDAY

_____
_____
_____

_____

⊙ SATURDAY / SUNDAY

_____
_____
_____

_____

DATES/WEEK OF:

AgendasRX

Organized – Saving Lives

○ MONDAY

PRIORITIES

_____

_____

○ TUESDAY

_____

_____

_____

○ WEDNESDAY

TO DO

_____

○ THURSDAY

_____

_____

_____

○ FRIDAY

_____

_____

○ SATURDAY / SUNDAY

_____

_____

DATES/WEEK OF:

AgendasRX

Organized – Saving Lives

_____

○ MONDAY

PRIORITIES

_____

_____

○ TUESDAY

_____

_____

_____

○ WEDNESDAY

TO DO

_____

_____

○ THURSDAY

_____

_____

_____

○ FRIDAY

_____

_____

_____

○ SATURDAY / SUNDAY

_____

_____

_____

DATES/WEEK OF:

AgendasRX

Organized ~ Saving Lives

_____

O MONDAY

PRIORITIES
_____

_____

O TUESDAY

_____

_____

_____

_____

_____

O WEDNESDAY

TO DO
_____

_____

_____

O THURSDAY

_____

_____

_____

_____

O FRIDAY

_____

_____

_____

_____

O SATURDAY / SUNDAY

_____

_____

_____

_____

_____

DATES/WEEK OF:

AgendasRX
Organized – Saving Lives

_____

○ MONDAY

PRIORITIES
_____
_____

○ TUESDAY
_____
_____
_____

○ WEDNESDAY

TO DO
_____

○ THURSDAY
_____
_____
_____

○ FRIDAY
_____
_____
_____

○ SATURDAY / SUNDAY
_____
_____
_____

DATES/WEEK OF:

AgendasRX
Organized – Saving Lives

⭕ MONDAY

PRIORITIES

_____

_____

⭕ TUESDAY

_____

_____

_____

⭕ WEDNESDAY

TO DO

_____

_____

⭕ THURSDAY

_____

_____

_____

⭕ FRIDAY

_____

_____

_____

⭕ SATURDAY / SUNDAY

_____

_____

_____

DATES/WEEK OF:

AgendasRX

Organized – Saving Lives

○ MONDAY

PRIORITIES

_____

_____

○ TUESDAY

_____

_____

_____

○ WEDNESDAY

TO DO

_____

○ THURSDAY

_____

_____

_____

_____

○ FRIDAY

_____

_____

_____

○ SATURDAY / SUNDAY

_____

_____

_____

DATES/WEEK OF:

AgendasRX

Organized – Saving Lives

○ MONDAY

PRIORITIES

_____

_____

○ TUESDAY

_____

_____

_____

○ WEDNESDAY

TO DO

_____

_____

○ THURSDAY

_____

_____

_____

○ FRIDAY

_____

_____

_____

○ SATURDAY / SUNDAY

_____

_____

_____

DATES/WEEK OF:

AgendasRX
Organized – Saving Lives

○ MONDAY

PRIORITIES

_____
_____
○ TUESDAY
_____
_____
_____

○ WEDNESDAY

TO DO

_____
_____
○ THURSDAY
_____
_____
_____

○ FRIDAY

_____
_____
_____
_____
○ SATURDAY / SUNDAY
_____
_____

DATES/WEEK OF:

AgendasRX
Organized ~ Saving Lives

○ MONDAY

_____

PRIORITIES

_____

○ TUESDAY

_____

_____

○ WEDNESDAY

_____

TO DO

_____

○ THURSDAY

_____

_____

○ FRIDAY

_____

_____

○ SATURDAY / SUNDAY

_____

_____

DATES/WEEK OF:

AgendasRX
Organized - Saving Lives

_____

○ MONDAY

PRIORITIES

_____

○ TUESDAY

_____

○ WEDNESDAY

TO DO

_____

○ THURSDAY

_____

○ FRIDAY

_____

○ SATURDAY / SUNDAY

_____

DATES/WEEK OF:

AgendasRX

Organized ~ Saving Lives

○ MONDAY

PRIORITIES

_____

_____

○ TUESDAY

_____

_____

_____

○ WEDNESDAY

TO DO

_____

○ THURSDAY

_____

_____

_____

○ FRIDAY

_____

_____

_____

○ SATURDAY / SUNDAY

_____

_____

_____

DATES/WEEK OF:

AgendasRX

Organized – Saving Lives

○ MONDAY

PRIORITIES

_____

_____

○ TUESDAY

_____

_____

_____

_____

○ WEDNESDAY

TO DO

_____

○ THURSDAY

_____

_____

_____

_____

○ FRIDAY

_____

_____

_____

○ SATURDAY / SUNDAY

_____

_____

_____

DATES/WEEK OF:

AgendasRX

Organized ~ Saving Lives

○ MONDAY

PRIORITIES

_____

_____

○ TUESDAY

_____

_____

_____

○ WEDNESDAY

TO DO

_____

_____

○ THURSDAY

_____

_____

_____

○ FRIDAY

_____

_____

○ SATURDAY / SUNDAY

_____

_____

_____

DATES/WEEK OF:

AgendasRX
Organized - Saving Lives

_____

○ MONDAY

PRIORITIES

_____

_____

○ TUESDAY
_____

_____

_____

_____

○ WEDNESDAY

TO DO

_____

_____

○ THURSDAY
_____

_____

_____

_____

○ FRIDAY
_____

_____

_____

_____

○ SATURDAY / SUNDAY
_____

_____

_____

DATES/WEEK OF:

AgendasRX
Organized – Saving Lives

○ MONDAY

PRIORITIES

_____

_____

○ TUESDAY

_____

_____

_____

○ WEDNESDAY

TO DO

_____

_____

○ THURSDAY

_____

_____

_____

○ FRIDAY

_____

_____

_____

○ SATURDAY / SUNDAY

_____

_____

_____

DATES/WEEK OF:

AgendasRX

Organized – Saving Lives

○ MONDAY

PRIORITIES

_____

_____

○ TUESDAY

_____

_____

_____

_____

○ WEDNESDAY

TO DO

_____

_____

○ THURSDAY

_____

_____

_____

_____

○ FRIDAY

_____

_____

_____

_____

○ SATURDAY / SUNDAY

_____

_____

_____

_____

DATES/WEEK OF:

AgendasRX
Organized – Saving Lives

O MONDAY

PRIORITIES

_____

_____

O TUESDAY

_____

_____

_____

O WEDNESDAY

TO DO

_____

O THURSDAY

_____

_____

_____

O FRIDAY

_____

_____

_____

O SATURDAY / SUNDAY

_____

_____

DATES/WEEK OF:

AgendasRX
Organized – Saving Lives

_____

○ MONDAY

PRIORITIES
_____
_____
○ TUESDAY
_____
_____
_____

○ WEDNESDAY

TO DO
_____
○ THURSDAY
_____
_____
_____

○ FRIDAY
_____
_____
_____

○ SATURDAY / SUNDAY
_____
_____
_____

DATES/WEEK OF:

AgendasRX
Organized − Saving Lives

○ MONDAY

PRIORITIES

_____

_____

○ TUESDAY

_____

_____

_____

○ WEDNESDAY

TO DO

_____

_____

○ THURSDAY

_____

_____

_____

_____

○ FRIDAY

_____

_____

_____

○ SATURDAY / SUNDAY

_____

_____

_____

DATES/WEEK OF:

AgendasRX
Organized - Saving Lives

○ MONDAY

PRIORITIES
_____
_____
○ TUESDAY
_____
_____
_____

○ WEDNESDAY

TO DO
_____
_____
○ THURSDAY
_____
_____
_____

○ FRIDAY
_____
_____
_____
_____
○ SATURDAY / SUNDAY
_____
_____
_____

DATES/WEEK OF:

AgendasRX
Organized – Saving Lives

○ MONDAY

PRIORITIES

○ TUESDAY

○ WEDNESDAY

TO DO

○ THURSDAY

○ FRIDAY

○ SATURDAY / SUNDAY

DATES/WEEK OF:

AgendasRX

Organized – Saving Lives

_____

○ MONDAY

PRIORITIES

_____

_____

○ TUESDAY

_____

_____

_____

_____

○ WEDNESDAY

TO DO

_____

_____

○ THURSDAY

_____

_____

_____

_____

○ FRIDAY

_____

_____

_____

_____

○ SATURDAY / SUNDAY

_____

_____

_____

DATES/WEEK OF:

AgendasRX
Organized – Saving Lives

_____

○ MONDAY

PRIORITIES
_____
_____
○ TUESDAY
_____
_____
_____
_____

○ WEDNESDAY

TO DO
_____
_____
○ THURSDAY
_____
_____
_____
_____

○ FRIDAY
_____
_____
_____

○ SATURDAY / SUNDAY
_____
_____

DATES/WEEK OF:

AgendasRX
Organized – Saving Lives

_____

○ MONDAY

PRIORITIES

_____

_____

_____

○ TUESDAY

_____

_____

_____

_____

_____

○ WEDNESDAY

TO DO

_____

_____

_____

○ THURSDAY

_____

_____

_____

_____

_____

○ FRIDAY

_____

_____

_____

_____

_____

○ SATURDAY / SUNDAY

_____

_____

_____

_____

_____

DATES/WEEK OF:

AgendasRX
Organized ~ Saving Lives

○ MONDAY

PRIORITIES

○ TUESDAY

○ WEDNESDAY

TO DO

○ THURSDAY

○ FRIDAY

○ SATURDAY / SUNDAY

DATES/WEEK OF:

AgendasRX

Organized – Saving Lives

_____

O MONDAY

PRIORITIES

_____
_____

O TUESDAY

_____
_____
_____

O WEDNESDAY

TO DO

_____
_____

O THURSDAY

_____
_____
_____
_____

O FRIDAY

_____
_____
_____
_____
_____

O SATURDAY / SUNDAY

_____
_____
_____

DATES/WEEK OF:

AgendasRX
Organized - Saving Lives

○ MONDAY

PRIORITIES

_____

_____

○ TUESDAY

_____

_____

_____

○ WEDNESDAY

TO DO

_____

○ THURSDAY

_____

_____

_____

○ FRIDAY

_____

_____

○ SATURDAY / SUNDAY

_____

_____

DATES/WEEK OF:

AgendasRX
Organized – Saving Lives

○ MONDAY

PRIORITIES
_____
_____
○ TUESDAY _____
_____
_____

○ WEDNESDAY
_____

TO DO
_____
_____
○ THURSDAY _____
_____
_____

○ FRIDAY _____
_____
_____
_____

○ SATURDAY / SUNDAY _____
_____
_____

DATES/WEEK OF:

AgendasRX
Organized – Saving Lives

O MONDAY

PRIORITIES

_____

_____

O TUESDAY

_____

_____

_____

_____

O WEDNESDAY

TO DO

_____

_____

O THURSDAY

_____

_____

_____

_____

O FRIDAY

_____

_____

_____

_____

O SATURDAY / SUNDAY

_____

_____

_____

DATES/WEEK OF:

AgendasRX

Organized — Saving Lives

_____

○ MONDAY

PRIORITIES
_____

_____

○ TUESDAY
_____

_____

_____

_____

○ WEDNESDAY

TO DO
_____

_____

_____

○ THURSDAY
_____

_____

_____

_____

_____

○ FRIDAY
_____

_____

_____

_____

○ SATURDAY / SUNDAY
_____

_____

_____

_____   _____

DATES/WEEK OF:

AgendasRX

Organized - Saving Lives

⭕ MONDAY

PRIORITIES

_____

_____

⭕ TUESDAY

_____

_____

_____

_____

⭕ WEDNESDAY

TO DO

_____

_____

⭕ THURSDAY

_____

_____

_____

_____

⭕ FRIDAY

_____

_____

_____

_____

⭕ SATURDAY / SUNDAY

_____

_____

_____

DATES/WEEK OF:

AgendasRX
Organized – Saving Lives

_____

O MONDAY

PRIORITIES

_____

_____

O TUESDAY   _____

_____

_____

_____

O WEDNESDAY

TO DO

_____

_____

O THURSDAY   _____

_____

_____

_____

O FRIDAY   _____

_____

_____

_____

_____

O SATURDAY / SUNDAY   _____

_____

_____

_____

DATES/WEEK OF:

AgendasRX
Organized – Saving Lives

O MONDAY

PRIORITIES

_____

_____

O TUESDAY

_____

_____

_____

_____

O WEDNESDAY

TO DO

_____

_____

O THURSDAY

_____

_____

_____

_____

O FRIDAY

_____

_____

_____

O SATURDAY / SUNDAY

_____

_____

_____

DATES/WEEK OF:

AgendasRX
Organized - Saving Lives

O MONDAY

PRIORITIES

_____

_____

O TUESDAY   _____

_____

_____

_____

O WEDNESDAY

TO DO

_____

_____

O THURSDAY   _____

_____

_____

_____

O FRIDAY   _____

_____

_____

_____

O SATURDAY / SUNDAY   _____

_____

_____

_____

DATES/WEEK OF:

AgendasRX

Organized - Saving Lives

⭕ MONDAY

PRIORITIES

⭕ TUESDAY

⭕ WEDNESDAY

TO DO

⭕ THURSDAY

⭕ FRIDAY

⭕ SATURDAY / SUNDAY

DATES/WEEK OF:

AgendasRX
Organized - Saving Lives

_____

○ MONDAY

PRIORITIES

_____

_____

○ TUESDAY

_____

_____

_____

_____

○ WEDNESDAY

TO DO

_____

_____

○ THURSDAY

_____

_____

_____

_____

○ FRIDAY

_____

_____

_____

○ SATURDAY / SUNDAY

_____

_____

_____

_____

DATES/WEEK OF:

AgendasRX
Organized – Saving Lives

○ MONDAY

PRIORITIES

○ TUESDAY

○ WEDNESDAY

TO DO

○ THURSDAY

○ FRIDAY

○ SATURDAY / SUNDAY

DATES/WEEK OF:

AgendasRX

Organized – Saving Lives

_____

O MONDAY

PRIORITIES

_____

O TUESDAY

_____

O WEDNESDAY

TO DO

_____

O THURSDAY

_____

O FRIDAY

_____

O SATURDAY / SUNDAY

_____

DATES/WEEK OF:

AgendasRX
Organized – Saving Lives

○ MONDAY

PRIORITIES

○ TUESDAY

○ WEDNESDAY

TO DO

○ THURSDAY

○ FRIDAY

○ SATURDAY / SUNDAY

DATES/WEEK OF:

AgendasRX
Organized - Saving Lives

○ MONDAY

_____

PRIORITIES

_____

_____

○ TUESDAY

_____

_____

_____

_____

_____

○ WEDNESDAY

_____

TO DO

_____

_____

○ THURSDAY

_____

_____

_____

_____

_____

○ FRIDAY

_____

_____

_____

_____

○ SATURDAY / SUNDAY

_____

_____

_____

_____

DATES/WEEK OF:

AgendasRX
Organized – Saving Lives

○ MONDAY

PRIORITIES

○ TUESDAY

○ WEDNESDAY

TO DO

○ THURSDAY

○ FRIDAY

○ SATURDAY / SUNDAY

DATES/WEEK OF:

AgendasRX
Organized – Saving Lives

_____

◯ MONDAY

_____

PRIORITIES

_____
_____
◯ TUESDAY
_____
_____
_____

_____

◯ WEDNESDAY

TO DO

_____
_____
_____
◯ THURSDAY
_____
_____
_____

_____
_____
◯ FRIDAY
_____
_____
_____

_____
_____
◯ SATURDAY / SUNDAY
_____
_____

_____
_____

DATES/WEEK OF:

AgendasRX
Organized - Saving Lives

○ MONDAY

PRIORITIES
_____
_____
○ TUESDAY
_____
_____
_____

○ WEDNESDAY

TO DO
_____
_____
○ THURSDAY
_____
_____
_____
_____

○ FRIDAY
_____
_____
_____

○ SATURDAY / SUNDAY
_____
_____
_____

DATES/WEEK OF:

AgendasRX
Organized – Saving Lives

_____

○ MONDAY

PRIORITIES

_____

_____
_____
○ TUESDAY
_____

_____

_____

_____

○ WEDNESDAY

TO DO

_____

_____

_____
○ THURSDAY
_____

_____

_____

_____

○ FRIDAY
_____

_____

_____

_____

○ SATURDAY / SUNDAY
_____

_____

_____

_____

DATES/WEEK OF:

AgendasRX
Organized – Saving Lives

○ MONDAY

PRIORITIES

_____

_____

○ TUESDAY

_____

_____

_____

_____

○ WEDNESDAY

TO DO

_____

_____

○ THURSDAY

_____

_____

_____

_____

○ FRIDAY

_____

_____

_____

○ SATURDAY / SUNDAY

_____

_____

_____

DATES/WEEK OF:

AgendasRX
Organized – Saving Lives

O MONDAY

PRIORITIES

_____

_____

O TUESDAY

_____

_____

_____

_____

O WEDNESDAY

TO DO

_____

O THURSDAY

_____

_____

_____

O FRIDAY

_____

_____

_____

_____

O SATURDAY / SUNDAY

_____

_____

_____

DATES/WEEK OF:

AgendasRX
Organized – Saving Lives

○ MONDAY

PRIORITIES

○ TUESDAY

○ WEDNESDAY

TO DO

○ THURSDAY

○ FRIDAY

○ SATURDAY / SUNDAY

DATES/WEEK OF:

AgendasRX
Organized – Saving Lives

_____

○ MONDAY

PRIORITIES

_____

_____

○ TUESDAY

_____

_____

_____

○ WEDNESDAY

TO DO

_____

_____

○ THURSDAY

_____

_____

_____

○ FRIDAY

_____

_____

_____

○ SATURDAY / SUNDAY

_____

_____

_____

DATES/WEEK OF:

AgendasRX
Organized ~ Saving Lives

_____

O MONDAY

PRIORITIES
_____
_____

O TUESDAY
_____
_____

_____

O WEDNESDAY

TO DO
_____
_____
_____

O THURSDAY
_____
_____

_____

O FRIDAY
_____
_____
_____

O SATURDAY / SUNDAY
_____
_____

_____

DATES/WEEK OF:

AgendasRX
Organized – Saving Lives

_____

○ MONDAY

PRIORITIES

_____
_____

○ TUESDAY
_____
_____
_____

○ WEDNESDAY

TO DO

_____
_____

○ THURSDAY
_____
_____
_____
_____

○ FRIDAY
_____
_____
_____
_____

○ SATURDAY / SUNDAY
_____
_____
_____

DATES/WEEK OF:

AgendasRX
Organized – Saving Lives

○ MONDAY

PRIORITIES

_____

_____

○ TUESDAY

_____

_____

_____

○ WEDNESDAY

TO DO

_____

○ THURSDAY

_____

_____

_____

○ FRIDAY

_____

_____

○ SATURDAY / SUNDAY

_____

_____

DATES/WEEK OF:

AgendasRX
Organized – Saving Lives

_____

O MONDAY

PRIORITIES

_____

_____

O TUESDAY

_____

_____

_____

O WEDNESDAY

TO DO

_____

O THURSDAY

_____

_____

_____

O FRIDAY

_____

_____

_____

O SATURDAY / SUNDAY

_____

_____

DATES/WEEK OF:

AgendasRX
Organized - Saving Lives

○ MONDAY

PRIORITIES

○ TUESDAY

○ WEDNESDAY

TO DO

○ THURSDAY

○ FRIDAY

○ SATURDAY / SUNDAY

DATES/WEEK OF:

AgendasRX
Organized – Saving Lives

O MONDAY

PRIORITIES

_____

_____

O TUESDAY

_____

_____

_____

O WEDNESDAY

TO DO

_____

_____

O THURSDAY

_____

_____

_____

_____

O FRIDAY

_____

_____

_____

_____

O SATURDAY / SUNDAY

_____

_____

_____

DATES/WEEK OF:

AgendasRX
Organized – Saving Lives

_____

○ MONDAY

PRIORITIES

_____

○ TUESDAY

_____

_____

_____

○ WEDNESDAY

TO DO

_____

_____

○ THURSDAY

_____

_____

_____

○ FRIDAY

_____

_____

_____

○ SATURDAY / SUNDAY

_____

_____

_____

DATES/WEEK OF:

AgendasRX
Organized — Saving Lives

_____

○ MONDAY

PRIORITIES

_____

_____

○ TUESDAY

_____

_____

_____

○ WEDNESDAY

TO DO

_____

_____

○ THURSDAY

_____

_____

_____

○ FRIDAY

_____

_____

_____

○ SATURDAY / SUNDAY

_____

_____

_____

DATES/WEEK OF:

AgendasRX
Organized – Saving Lives

⭕ MONDAY

PRIORITIES

_____

⭕ TUESDAY

_____

_____

⭕ WEDNESDAY

TO DO

_____

⭕ THURSDAY

_____

_____

_____

⭕ FRIDAY

_____

_____

⭕ SATURDAY / SUNDAY

_____

_____

DATES/WEEK OF:

AgendasRX

Organized − Saving Lives

_____

○ MONDAY

PRIORITIES

_____

_____

○ TUESDAY

_____

_____

_____

○ WEDNESDAY

TO DO

_____

_____

○ THURSDAY

_____

_____

_____

○ FRIDAY

_____

_____

_____

○ SATURDAY / SUNDAY

_____

_____

DATES/WEEK OF:

AgendasRX
Organized - Saving Lives

○ MONDAY

PRIORITIES
_____
_____
○ TUESDAY
_____
_____
_____
_____

○ WEDNESDAY

TO DO
_____
_____
_____
○ THURSDAY
_____
_____
_____
_____

○ FRIDAY
_____
_____
_____
_____

○ SATURDAY / SUNDAY
_____
_____
_____

DATES/WEEK OF:

AgendasRX
Organized - Saving Lives

_____

O MONDAY

PRIORITIES

_____

_____

O TUESDAY

_____

_____

_____

_____

O WEDNESDAY

_____

TO DO

_____

_____

O THURSDAY

_____

_____

_____

_____

O FRIDAY

_____

_____

_____

_____

O SATURDAY / SUNDAY

_____

_____

_____

DATES/WEEK OF:

AgendasRX
Organized - Saving Lives

O MONDAY

PRIORITIES

_____

_____

O TUESDAY

_____

_____

_____

O WEDNESDAY

TO DO

_____

_____

O THURSDAY

_____

_____

_____

_____

O FRIDAY

_____

_____

_____

O SATURDAY / SUNDAY

_____

_____

_____

DATES/WEEK OF:

AgendasRX
Organized - Saving Lives

_____

O MONDAY

PRIORITIES
_____
_____
O TUESDAY
_____
_____
_____
_____

O WEDNESDAY

TO DO
_____
_____
O THURSDAY
_____
_____
_____
_____
_____
O FRIDAY
_____
_____
_____
_____
O SATURDAY / SUNDAY
_____
_____
_____

DATES/WEEK OF:

AgendasRX
Organized – Saving Lives

_____

○ MONDAY

PRIORITIES
_____
_____
○ TUESDAY
_____
_____
_____

○ WEDNESDAY

TO DO
_____
_____
○ THURSDAY
_____
_____
_____

○ FRIDAY
_____
_____
_____

○ SATURDAY / SUNDAY
_____
_____
_____

DATES/WEEK OF:

AgendasRX

Organized – Saving Lives

_____

○ MONDAY

PRIORITIES

_____

_____

○ TUESDAY

_____

_____

_____

_____

○ WEDNESDAY

TO DO

_____

_____

○ THURSDAY

_____

_____

_____

_____

○ FRIDAY

_____

_____

_____

_____

○ SATURDAY / SUNDAY

_____

_____

_____

DATES/WEEK OF:

AgendasRX
Organized – Saving Lives

_____

O MONDAY

PRIORITIES
_____
_____
O TUESDAY
_____
_____
_____
_____
_____

O WEDNESDAY

TO DO
_____
_____
_____
O THURSDAY
_____
_____
_____
_____
_____

O FRIDAY
_____
_____
_____
_____

O SATURDAY / SUNDAY
_____
_____
_____

AgendasRX

Organized + Saving Lives

NOTES | THOUGHTS | IDEAS

TRUST YOUR *crazy* IDEAS

TRUST
YOUR
crazy
IDEAS

TRUST YOUR crazy IDEAS

TRUST YOUR crazy IDEAS

TRUST YOUR crazy IDEAS

TRUST YOUR crazy IDEAS

AgendasRX

Organized + Saving Lives

HABITS TRACKER

Habit Tracker

Month _____

Year _____

Day															
1															
2															
3															
4															
5															
6															
7															
8															
9															
10															
11															
12															
13															
14															
15															
16															
17															
18															
19															
20															
21															
22															
23															
24															
25															
26															
27															
28															
29															
30															
31															

Habit Tracker

Month _____

Year _____

Day													
1													
2													
3													
4													
5													
6													
7													
8													
9													
10													
11													
12													
13													
14													
15													
16													
17													
18													
19													
20													
21													
22													
23													
24													
25													
26													
27													
28													
29													
30													
31													

Habit Tracker

Month _____

Year _____

Day															
1															
2															
3															
4															
5															
6															
7															
8															
9															
10															
11															
12															
13															
14															
15															
16															
17															
18															
19															
20															
21															
22															
23															
24															
25															
26															
27															
28															
29															
30															
31															

Habit Tracker

Month _____

Year _____

Day													
1													
2													
3													
4													
5													
6													
7													
8													
9													
10													
11													
12													
13													
14													
15													
16													
17													
18													
19													
20													
21													
22													
23													
24													
25													
26													
27													
28													
29													
30													
31													

Habit Tracker

Month _____

Year _____

Day															
1															
2															
3															
4															
5															
6															
7															
8															
9															
10															
11															
12															
13															
14															
15															
16															
17															
18															
19															
20															
21															
22															
23															
24															
25															
26															
27															
28															
29															
30															
31															

Habit Tracker

Month _____

Year _____

Day													
1													
2													
3													
4													
5													
6													
7													
8													
9													
10													
11													
12													
13													
14													
15													
16													
17													
18													
19													
20													
21													
22													
23													
24													
25													
26													
27													
28													
29													
30													
31													

Habit Tracker

Month _____

Year _____

Day													
1													
2													
3													
4													
5													
6													
7													
8													
9													
10													
11													
12													
13													
14													
15													
16													
17													
18													
19													
20													
21													
22													
23													
24													
25													
26													
27													
28													
29													
30													
31													

Habit Tracker

Month _____

Year _____

Day															
1															
2															
3															
4															
5															
6															
7															
8															
9															
10															
11															
12															
13															
14															
15															
16															
17															
18															
19															
20															
21															
22															
23															
24															
25															
26															
27															
28															
29															
30															
31															

Habit Tracker

Month _____

Year _____

Day													
1													
2													
3													
4													
5													
6													
7													
8													
9													
10													
11													
12													
13													
14													
15													
16													
17													
18													
19													
20													
21													
22													
23													
24													
25													
26													
27													
28													
29													
30													
31													

Habit Tracker

Month _____

Year _____

Day														
1														
2														
3														
4														
5														
6														
7														
8														
9														
10														
11														
12														
13														
14														
15														
16														
17														
18														
19														
20														
21														
22														
23														
24														
25														
26														
27														
28														
29														
30														
31														

Habit Tracker

Month _____

Year _____

Day														
1														
2														
3														
4														
5														
6														
7														
8														
9														
10														
11														
12														
13														
14														
15														
16														
17														
18														
19														
20														
21														
22														
23														
24														
25														
26														
27														
28														
29														
30														
31														

Habit Tracker

Month _____

Year _____

Day														
1														
2														
3														
4														
5														
6														
7														
8														
9														
10														
11														
12														
13														
14														
15														
16														
17														
18														
19														
20														
21														
22														
23														
24														
25														
26														
27														
28														
29														
30														
31														

AgendasRX

Organized + Saving Lives

CONTACTS LIST

contacts

FIRST NAME

LAST NAME

HOME PHONE

WORK PHONE

ORGANIZATION

RELATIONSHIP

E-MAIL ADDRESS

FIRST NAME

LAST NAME

HOME PHONE

WORK PHONE

ORGANIZATION

RELATIONSHIP

E-MAIL ADDRESS

FIRST NAME

LAST NAME

HOME PHONE

WORK PHONE

ORGANIZATION

RELATIONSHIP

E-MAIL ADDRESS

contacts

FIRST NAME

LAST NAME

HOME PHONE

WORK PHONE

ORGANIZATION

RELATIONSHIP

E-MAIL ADDRESS

FIRST NAME

LAST NAME

HOME PHONE

WORK PHONE

ORGANIZATION

RELATIONSHIP

E-MAIL ADDRESS

FIRST NAME

LAST NAME

HOME PHONE

WORK PHONE

ORGANIZATION

RELATIONSHIP

E-MAIL ADDRESS

contacts

FIRST NAME

LAST NAME

HOME PHONE

WORK PHONE

ORGANIZATION

RELATIONSHIP

E-MAIL ADDRESS

FIRST NAME

LAST NAME

HOME PHONE

WORK PHONE

ORGANIZATION

RELATIONSHIP

E-MAIL ADDRESS

FIRST NAME

LAST NAME

HOME PHONE

WORK PHONE

ORGANIZATION

RELATIONSHIP

E-MAIL ADDRESS

contacts

FIRST NAME

LAST NAME

HOME PHONE

WORK PHONE

ORGANIZATION

RELATIONSHIP

E-MAIL ADDRESS

FIRST NAME

LAST NAME

HOME PHONE

WORK PHONE

ORGANIZATION

RELATIONSHIP

E-MAIL ADDRESS

FIRST NAME

LAST NAME

HOME PHONE

WORK PHONE

ORGANIZATION

RELATIONSHIP

E-MAIL ADDRESS

contacts

FIRST NAME   LAST NAME

HOME PHONE   WORK PHONE

ORGANIZATION   RELATIONSHIP

E-MAIL ADDRESS

FIRST NAME   LAST NAME

HOME PHONE   WORK PHONE

ORGANIZATION   RELATIONSHIP

E-MAIL ADDRESS

FIRST NAME   LAST NAME

HOME PHONE   WORK PHONE

ORGANIZATION   RELATIONSHIP

E-MAIL ADDRESS

contacts

FIRST NAME   LAST NAME

HOME PHONE   WORK PHONE

ORGANIZATION   RELATIONSHIP

E-MAIL ADDRESS

FIRST NAME   LAST NAME

HOME PHONE   WORK PHONE

ORGANIZATION   RELATIONSHIP

E-MAIL ADDRESS

FIRST NAME   LAST NAME

HOME PHONE   WORK PHONE

ORGANIZATION   RELATIONSHIP

E-MAIL ADDRESS

contacts

FIRST NAME

LAST NAME

HOME PHONE

WORK PHONE

ORGANIZATION

RELATIONSHIP

E-MAIL ADDRESS

FIRST NAME

LAST NAME

HOME PHONE

WORK PHONE

ORGANIZATION

RELATIONSHIP

E-MAIL ADDRESS

FIRST NAME

LAST NAME

HOME PHONE

WORK PHONE

ORGANIZATION

RELATIONSHIP

E-MAIL ADDRESS

contacts

FIRST NAME

LAST NAME

HOME PHONE

WORK PHONE

ORGANIZATION

RELATIONSHIP

E-MAIL ADDRESS

FIRST NAME

LAST NAME

HOME PHONE

WORK PHONE

ORGANIZATION

RELATIONSHIP

E-MAIL ADDRESS

FIRST NAME

LAST NAME

HOME PHONE

WORK PHONE

ORGANIZATION

RELATIONSHIP

E-MAIL ADDRESS

AgendasRX

Organized + Saving Lives

Made in the USA
Middletown, DE
05 February 2023

24050435R00087